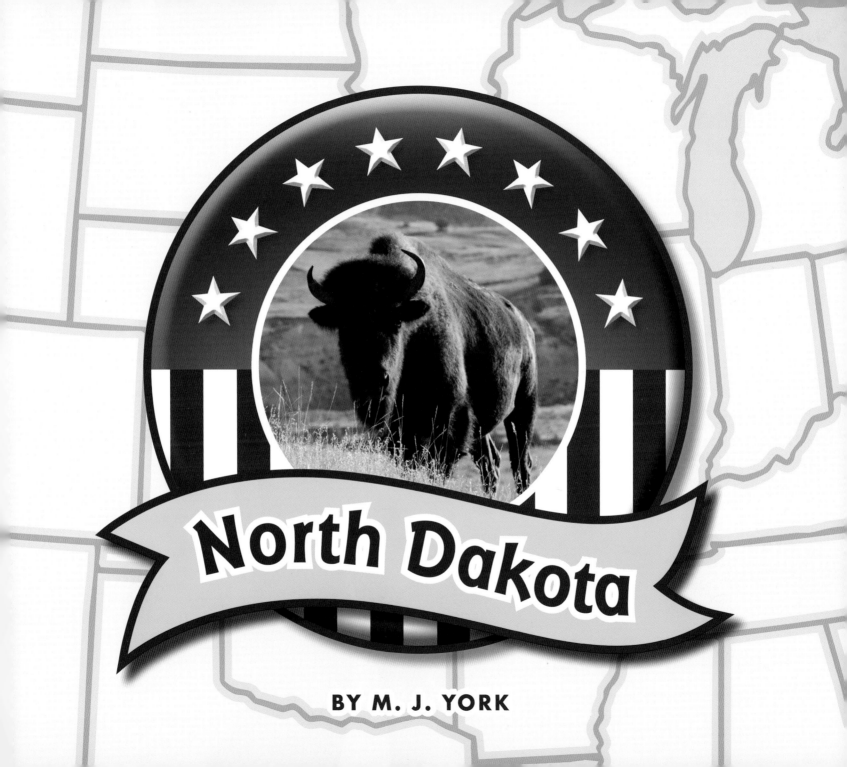

North Dakota

BY M. J. YORK

The Child's World

Published by The Child's World®
1980 Lookout Drive • Mankato, MN 56003-1705
800-599-READ • www.childsworld.com

ACKNOWLEDGMENTS
The Child's World®: Mary Berendes, Publishing Director
The Design Lab: Design and production
Red Line Editorial: Editorial direction

PHOTO CREDITS: Eric Foltz/iStockphoto, cover, 1, 3; Matt Kania/Map
Hero, Inc., 4, 5; iStockphoto, 7, 10; Bill Koplitz/iStockphoto, 9; Jim Jurica/
iStockphoto, 11; Keith Crowley/iStockphoto, 13; North Wind Picture
Archives/Photolibrary, 15; Chuck Haney/Photolibrary, 17; AP Images, 19;
Beverley Vycital/iStockphoto, 21; One Mile Up, 22; Quarter-dollar coin
image from the United States Mint, 22

LIBRARY OF CONGRESS CATALOGING-IN-PUBLICATION DATA
York, M. J., 1983–
  North Dakota / by M.J. York.
    p. cm.
  Includes bibliographical references and index.
  ISBN 978-1-60253-478-0 (library bound : alk. paper)
  1. North Dakota—Juvenile literature. I. Title.

F636.3.Y67 2010
978.4—dc22

2010019262

Printed in the United States of America in Mankato, Minnesota.
July 2010
F11538

On the cover:
A bison roams
in Theodore
Roosevelt
National Park.

CONTENTS

Geography

Let's explore North Dakota! North Dakota is in the north-central part of the United States. This area is called the Midwest. North Dakota shares its northern border with Canada.

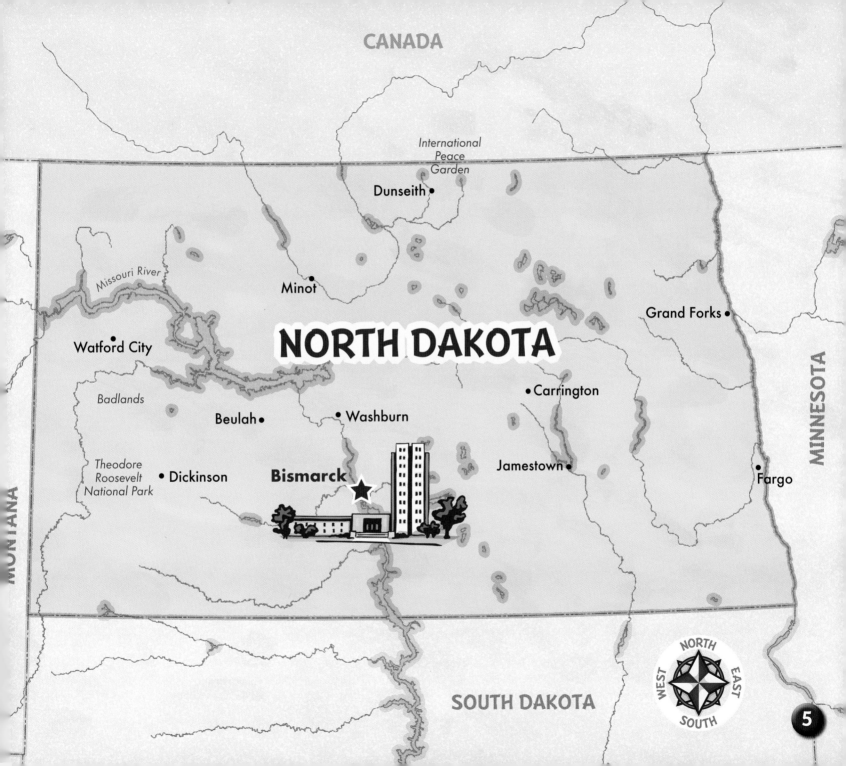

CANADA

International Peace Garden

Dunseith •

Minot •

Grand Forks •

NORTH DAKOTA

Missouri River

Watford City •

Carrington •

Badlands

Beulah •

• Washburn

Theodore Roosevelt National Park

• Dickinson

Bismarck ★

Jamestown •

Fargo •

MONTANA

MINNESOTA

SOUTH DAKOTA

NORTH
WEST   EAST
SOUTH

Cities

Bismarck is the capital of North Dakota. Fargo is the largest city in the state. Grand Forks and Minot are other well-known cities.

More than 58,000 people live in Bismarck. ▶

7

Land

North Dakota has large areas of **prairies**. These areas are part of the Great **Plains**. The **Badlands** are in the west. The ground in this area is bad for farming. The Badlands have beautiful rock **formations**. The Missouri River runs through the state.

American bison roam on North Dakota's sweeping prairies. ▶

8

The Great Plains spread across the central and western United States.

Plants and Animals

The state bird of North Dakota is the western meadowlark. It has brown spots and a yellow chest. The state flower is the wild prairie rose. The state grass is western wheatgrass.

Western wheatgrass covered almost all of North Dakota before people began farming the land.

The wild prairie rose grows in fields and meadows throughout North Dakota. ▶

People and Work

Almost 650,000 people live in North Dakota. Many people work on farms and **ranches**. Farmers grow wheat, corn, and soybeans. Ranchers raise cattle. Oil drilling and **windmills** are becoming important in the state.

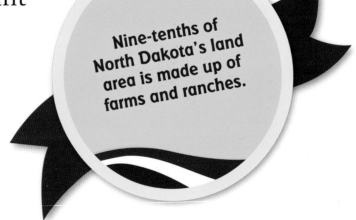

Nine-tenths of North Dakota's land area is made up of farms and ranches.

These large machines use the wind to make energy. ▶

History

Native Americans have lived in the North Dakota area for thousands of years. Some built villages. Others followed the animals they hunted. People from Europe came to the area in the 1700s. They traded furs with Native Americans. The United States claimed the land in 1803. North Dakota became the thirty-ninth state on November 2, 1889.

The Mandans lived in the area that is now North Dakota. ▶

15

Ways of Life

Many North Dakotans enjoy the outdoors. People enjoy bird watching here. They ride horses and bikes on the Maah Daah Hey Trail. People also **hike** and hunt.

A man rides a mountain bike on North Dakota's Sully Creek Trail. ▶

Famous People

Sacagawea is a famous North Dakotan from long ago. She was a member of the Shoshone **tribe**. She met explorers Meriwether Lewis and William Clark in 1804. She became their guide. She helped them reach the Pacific Ocean.

Baseball player Roger Maris grew up in Fargo, North Dakota. Television entertainer Lawrence Welk was born and raised in North Dakota.

Roger Maris set a home-run record when he played for the New York Yankees. ▶

Famous Places

Many people visit North Dakota to explore Theodore Roosevelt National Park. They hike in the Badlands. They see bison, prairie dogs, and wild horses. The **International** Peace Garden stands for friendship between the United States and Canada. It is on the border between the countries. Each year, gardeners here create **designs** using colorful flowers.

Wild horses run through Theodore Roosevelt National Park. ▶

State Symbols

Seal

North Dakota's state seal has a Native American, a bison, and a tree on it. These stand for North Dakota's history and nature. Go to childsworld.com/links for a link to North Dakota's state Web site, where you can get a firsthand look at the state seal.

Flag

The state flag shows an eagle with arrows in its claws. The flag is the same as the flag of a North Dakota army group.

Quarter

North Dakota's state quarter shows two bison and the setting sun. The quarter came out in 2006.

Glossary

Badlands (BAD-landz): Badlands are areas of land with rock formations, few plants, and little soil. The Badlands are in western North Dakota.

designs (dih-ZYNZ): Designs are drawings or shapes. Gardeners at the International Peace Garden create designs using flowers.

entertainer (en-tur-TAYN-ur): An entertainer is a person who makes others laugh or enjoy something. Famous entertainer Lawrence Welk was born and raised in North Dakota.

formations (for-MAY-shunz): Formations are shapes. The Badlands have beautiful rock formations.

hike (HYK): To hike is to take a walk in a natural area, such as a hill or a mountain. People can hike in North Dakota's Badlands.

international (in-tur-NASH-uh-nul): International means something involving many countries. The International Peace Garden in North Dakota stands for friendship.

plains (PLAYNZ): Plains are areas of flat land that do not have many trees. Part of North Dakota is the Great Plains.

prairies (PRAYR-eez): Prairies are flat or hilly grasslands. Part of North Dakota is prairies.

ranches (RANCH-ez): Ranches are large farms for raising cattle or other large animals. North Dakota has many ranches.

seal (SEEL): A seal is a symbol a state uses for government business. North Dakota's state seal shows items that stand for the state's history and nature.

symbols (SIM-bulz): Symbols are pictures or things that stand for something else. North Dakota's seal and flag are symbols for the state.

tribe (TRYB): A tribe is a group of people who share ancestors and customs. Sacagawea was part of the Shoshone tribe.

windmills (WIHND-milz): Windmills are machines that use the wind to make power. North Dakota has windmills on its land.

Further Information

Books

Keller, Laurie. *The Scrambled States of America*. New York: Henry Holt, 2002.

Salonen, Roxane B. *P is for Peace Garden: A North Dakota Alphabet*. Chelsea, MI: Sleeping Bear Press, 2005.

Zollman, Pam. *North Dakota*. New York: Children's Press, 2005.

Web Sites

Visit our Web site for links about North Dakota: *childsworld.com/links*

Note to Parents, Teachers, and Librarians: We routinely verify our Web links to make sure they are safe and active sites. So encourage your readers to check them out!

Index